This is Kate.

Kate loves to skate.

Kate loves to skate and
chase and race.

Kate loves to skate from
place to place.

Wait, Kate!

See Jake race!

Did Jake take the cake
Kate baked?

Skate, Kate, skate!

Take the cake from Jake!

Kate raced on skates.

Skate, Kate, skate!

Jake was chased and
chased.

Kate chased Jake from place to place.

Kate got Jake by the
lake . . .

with the plate and the
cake she baked.

Kate and Jake ate!